More Than Words

Poems & Sketches

Meadowlark Press, LLC
meadowlark-books.com
P.O. Box 333, Emporia, KS 66801

More Than Words: Poems & Sketches
Copyright ©Kevin Rabas, 2021

All rights reserved. This book or any portion thereof may not be reproduced or used in any manner whatsoever without the express written permission of the author, except for the use of brief quotations in a book review.

Cover photo by Becky Provost Roper
Author photo by Dave Leiker
Cover design by Eric Sonnakolb
Interior design by Linzi Garcia

ISBN: 978-1-7362232-1-5

Library of Congress Control Number: 2020953029

Praise for *More Than Words*

More Than Words finds its guiding spirit in the jazz aficionado who, told by management not to tape a Charlie Parker gig, sneaks a cord into a bathroom stall and listens rapt with headphones on the toilet seat. The poems in this generous collection relish the outsiders of the world, from the bullied middle schooler to the struggling parent, the haunted jazzmen to their haunted fans. This is art without ego, ending in an incantation for readers: "whatever it is / I ask you / to hold on." What keeps you going? I don't know. But you are holding onto this book now, and you would do well to praise your luck.
 —Michael Miller, author of *Angels in Seven*

Kevin Rabas's poems are as honest as an open prairie, as fierce as the inner city, and as cool as the jazz that pulses through every verse. He explores vast spaces beneath big skies and digs into sidewalk cracks under street lamps in his ongoing quest to uncover the heartbeats, the rhythms, of our souls.
 —Michael D. Graves, author of *All Hallows' Shadows* and other
  Pete Stone mysteries

These poems and sketches by Kevin Rabas are deceptive in their apparent straightforward unadorned language . . . Even though it is dark in its depiction, the collection ends with a hopeful note . . . when the author asks readers "to hold on." *More Than Words* reveals wise insights about human nature.
 —Silvia Kofler, poet and editor of *Thorny Locust*

Kansas Poet Laureate Emeritus Kevin Rabas's new collection is *More Than Words* in more ways than one. Chronicling love, pain, and the past while anticipating a future that "burns burns / above" what we know, this seasoned teacher and jazz drummer lays out life moments like short, sharp snare rolls: riffs on fatherhood, childhood, music, myth, and marriage. In these potent poems Rabas distills to its essence the world he inhabits, "a man in the woods / with a mic / capturing birdsong."
 —Tyler Robert Sheldon, editor-in-chief of *MockingHeart Review*
  and author of *Driving Together*

If a form of synesthesia is hearing music and seeing a poem or seeing life and associating it with a beat, then Rabas has perfected his observation of the mundane and the magnificent with astounding rhythmical and lyrical depiction. To open *More Than Words* is to enter a symphony of life.
 —Ronda Miller, former president of Kansas Authors Club (2018-
  2019), author of five books of poetry, including *MoonStain*
  and *WaterSigns*

More Than Words

Poems & Sketches by
Kevin Rabas

Meadowlark Press, LLC
Emporia, Kansas USA

Also by Kevin Rabas

POETRY COLLECTIONS
Watch Your Head (Kellogg P, 2020)
On Drums (Woodley P, 2019)
Everyone Just Wants to Drum (Spartan P, 2019)
Like Buddha-Calm Bird (Meadowlark P, 2018)
Late for Cymbal Line (Local Gems P, 2017)
All That Jazz (Spartan P, 2017)
Sonny Kenner's Red Guitar (Coal City Review P, 2013)
Lisa's Flying Electric Piano (Woodley P, 2009)
Bird's Horn (Coal City Review P, 2007)

POETRY CHAPBOOKS
Bird Book (Analog Submission P, 2020)
Eliot's Violin (Oil Hill P, 2015)

POETRY & STORIES
Songs for My Father (Meadowlark P, 2016)

POETRY & PLAYS
Watch Your Head 2 (Kellogg P, 2020)

NOVELS/NOVELLAS
Elizabeth's City (Spartan P, 2020)
Green Bike (with Graves & Simmons)
(Meadowlark P, 2014)

SHORT STORY COLLECTIONS
Spider Face (Otoliths, 2011)

EDITED ANTHOLOGIES
Kansas Letters to a Young Poet (Bluestem P, 2020)
Bards Against Hunger: Kansas (Local Gems P, 2018)

For Lisa

More Than Words

Our Nature
Thanksgiving 3
[flat] 4
On a Wire 5
[Cicada Song] 6
Drink enough tea 7
That sweat 8
Mop Up 9
Parked Car 10
Thick Paint 11
[No one notices] 12
[Purple Drops] 13
Long After the Dirty Thirties 14
Twilight 15
[about those purple mountains
    on the Kansas state seal] 16
These trees 17
Autumn Sidewalk 18
[ready] 19
Fire 20
Dry Summer 21
[My feet know] 22
[lifelong song] 23
Saguaro 24
[a rustle of leaves] 25
Leaf Music 26
[about the bees] 27

Music
[Opening Band] 31
Rain Date 32
[Kaboom] 33
[so we stay home] 34
[The saxophonist] 35
Improv 36
Neon Above All of the Clubs 37
[that dance band] 38
Bird at the Jelly Joint, Fall 1938 39
Bird Watcher 40

Recording Bird from the Can 41
at massey hall 42
Bird's Table 43
Bird at 100 44
[Sax Man] 45
At the Bar, Casey's 46
Open Mic with Music 47
[Older Drummer] 48
The Basie Way 49
[how it ended] 50
[Chops] 51
Tadd Dameron leaves a note 52

Growing Up
[swingset] 55
Treasure 56
Walking Trail, Holiday Lights, Lenexa 57
When I Grow Up 58
Gifted 59
Pop Out King 60
Fourth Grade 61
Dunked 62
About that time we left the locker room
    through a cloud 63
[My pits itch] 64
Injured in Band 65
Guard 66
[handbill shot] 67
Trampoline 68
Ready Player One 69
[Inner Kid] 70
[our neighborhood] 71
[lugging] 72
Group Blast 73
The Red Balloon 74

Romance
Always Good 77
Catherine & Hal 78
Rogue 79
And the Ring 80

In the Pocket 81
Hug 82
Preacher Couple 83
More Than Words 84
[say anything, or senior year break-up] 85
Sauce 86
Lisa, my darling, ... 87
Plaza, Eastern Edge 88
Happy Birthday 89
Night Out, Away 90
L on Piano 91
On Paper 92

Sickness
[driving all night] 95
Andy's Blues 96
At the Short Stop Gas Station 97
[corona—stage one] 98
[unintended birthday gift] 99
[it's here] 100
[love in the time of coronavirus #1] 101
[love in the time of coronavirus #2] 102
[in our cave] 103
[the box] 104
[how to work from home] 105
Sunday, 12 April 2020 106
Cellphone, Palmed 107
[how we use our space] 108
[rumination] 109
[dying favor] 110
[for George Floyd] 111
[RE: the taunting of Nathan Phillips,
   Omaha Elder] 112
Kobach on Parade 113
Pitchforks 114
[hold on] 115

Acknowledgments & Note 117
Current Influences 118
Words of Thanks 120
About the Author 121

A Preliminary Thought

Whatever my life is, I've tried to write it. I've tried to show you some of what I know so that you don't have to live the bad and so that you can take warmth from the good and know there is so much light out there, both from the sun and from far beyond, like light from a distant star. That light has come a long long way this night, and, like hope, it's there, shining, and, if you take great care and look, you can always see that white spark against the dark.

—Kevin Rabas, Saturday, 17 Oct. 2020, 11 PM

Our Nature

Thanksgiving

Our neighbors say
   come over today,
Thanksgiving, and so
we are no longer alone—
and eat rice goldened
   with saffron*
and raise wine
to friendship, both new and lasting,
clank glass and spatter blood orange
droplets—and spend an evening hovering
over a board game, *Settlers*
of Catan, and although we
build roads and armies, no one
builds walls, and we trade, barter
cards, while our young sons
swing Styrofoam swords
   in the front yard,
the sun sinking
   around, and tomorrow
or Saturday, they say
   snow and tons of it,
and I think ahead months
to how it all ends
in this part of the country:
   the crocus poke through
   the snow, throw
   back their bonnets,
   and eye the sun.

---

*saffron: crocus pollen

[flat]

How the dog
flattens himself
to go under
the neighbor's fence.
It's hard, but not
that hard

to leave.

On a Wire

The murder
keeps quiet
in the cold.
Those crows.

[Cicada Song]

Outside, cicada song,
the green evening going
grey. I've been inside
all day.

Drink enough tea
  and you'll have to
piss and piss, think only
of your own water
and that little balloon
beneath your gut.

That sweat
that runs down your back streams
   along the spine. Stand out
in the summer sun long enough,
   and you'll see
how much water
   you're made of.

Mop Up

Truckstop
   stores their stuff
in the bright room
   behind the stage,
come in
   out of hard rain
and wring
   their hair,
puddles
   up front.

RE: The band Truckstop Honeymoon

Parked Car

Rain on my windshield,
a splattering, like Pollock
paint, like coins, like bugs
come to rest.

Thick Paint

At the edge
  of the board,
there's a shadow
  the paint makes,
like petals
  on the walk
after rain.

RE: Allison Schulnik's painting "Skipping Skeletons"

[No one notices]

I.
No one notices
  the sky
enough
  when they run.

II.
But I've seen
  tomorrow
coming, going,
a white line.

III.
Where will
  we go
when we can
  no longer
run, when I
  no longer
have you
    to follow?

RE: Allison Schulnik's painting "Skipping Skeletons"

[Purple Drops]

Outside, the sky's gone
   green. The weed whip line
is in bits at the lawn's fringe, almost
   a nest, and the machine
is on the sidewalk where it stopped.
   Down comes the rain
in purple drops.

Long After the Dirty Thirties

During storms, Grandma
would still stuff wet towels
into the window
sills, remembering when
the dust would come.

Twilight

Sun
just under, the sky
bluing, purpling, summer
in a small town by the highway,
the cars going, going by.

**[about those purple mountains
  on the Kansas state seal]**

When it's cool enough evenings
    for a jacket,
we call it Colorado
    weather, and we dream
of the state just to the west of us,
the one full of mountains.

These trees
they green
when August sun
goes white hot
and dries the rain
and withers the grass
around.

Autumn Sidewalk

The leaf
across the walk
is a yellow
   five-pointed star
like a blessing
   from the branches
like a report card
   stamp: A+
all over the university
   this yes yes yes
come on over
and walk across
   my fall carpet
you too
   can be a star.

[ready]

Lawn mown,
I am ready, sky.
Erupt.

Fire

Some say
hell is full
of fire, and we
should hate
the flame,
but I love
those orange fingers,
red and yellow
mountains, that reach
for the moon.

Dry Summer

That afternoon, clouds,
the broken promise
of rain. Wind
that blows clouds
across and along.
The yellow grasses,
like supplicants, bent
over.

[My feet know]

That night, the stars
   like a breadcrumb trail,
   my hand on the envelope
   as I walk to my mailbox,
   eyes up. My feet know
   the way.

[lifelong song]

I like how the birds sing, rain
or no rain, how their lives
are filled with their own
song, own notes.

Saguaro*

Each limb took
  some one hundred
years to grow—
rooted, planted in sand,
  the view: miles
and miles, flat.
(And will we ever
  get back?)

*saguaro: person-shaped, tall cactus

[a rustle of leaves]

They take
a lot of water—
the cottonwoods,
but in return
in wind
they sound
oceanic.

Leaf Music

How the wind moves
  the leaves, each leaf
like a note on the staff—
  a quick, busy run,
16th and 32nd notes all over
  and beyond
the 5 lines.

[about the bees]

14 April 2013, 1 PM

Dear Dad,

I did what you said about the bees. I put a cardboard box with handles out in the yard under the bees. I put the cotton balls in after soaking them in lemon extract, like you said. The swarm mobbed the branch, like a fire on the pine, bees like sparks, buzzing paths around the thick, nut-like cluster, hundreds upon hundreds of bodies and wings. Eliot and his friend wouldn't go out at first, but I told them they're not interested in boys with sticks. They just want a new home.

The wind's picking up, and the clouds are like grey charcoal sticks, thick. Lisa and I got out the ladder. She held it, and I cleaned out the gutters, leaves and shingle grit, like wet sand clumps. We don't want the gutters to overflow and dump onto the house. You know what I mean. More later. Any advice? The lemon balls don't seem to be working.

Love,
Kevin

****

1:20 PM
Son,

Try honey. Drizzle it inside on one wall of the box.

****

1:40 PM

Dad,
The honey seems to be working. Bees are going into the box. There's still a thick mob of bees on the branch, but about 10 bees are on the box, and more are most likely inside.

Eliot's no longer afraid. I guess at 9, if you don't get stung at once, you return to the trampoline. Once I get the bees in the box, do you want the box?

Love,
Kevin

****

2:30 PM

Yes. Those bees are worth $200. I'll be by tonight around dinner time. I'll bring a bucket of chicken.

Music

[Opening Band]

Much like
that bad band switch joke
"Where's Fluffy" plays
  in *Nick and Norah's*,
there's a teen
  with his fat foot
in the kick drum, bombing us
instead of folky Truckstop
  Honeymoon, and he sticks
a flurry of sixteenth notes
across all his toms
  to seal it: this
ain't folk
to open.

Rain Date

Halfway through
the sound check,
and they ask the bass to play,
and he riffs the first underworld
level in Super Mario, including
a few high, tinny
coin hits, my son's
middle school music teacher
   up on the stand
   with his band
   on a school night,
opening act for an out-
of-town act, brought in
by the rain.

[Kaboom]

The only time
   I've been part
of anything oceanic vast,
whole whale big, was once
   on drum with the orchestra,
tufted mallet in hand,
   on a tune where
I played this one-note
   solo, kaboom.

[so we stay home]

So we stay home
watch the rain:
gray day, the lawn greening,
the yellow crocus up, trumpeting—
and nowhere to go, no one
to meet for lunch, the bug
in the background, and so
I listen to Mingus, "Goodbye
Pork Pie Hat," and pray
for my parents
in another town
and for jazz musicians, out
of work, home with their saxes
and drums, rumbling somewhere,
like the Italian tenor, singing
from his window to an empty
empty street.

Wednesday, 18 March 2020, Emporia, Kansas

[The saxophonist]

I.
The saxophonist
introduces the band,
says, "Now, let's see
if my horn's gone cold,"
puts the reed
to his lips, blows.
"No."

II.
The man on
   clarinet
points at who
   goes next,
fours, back
   and forth
with the drums,
   one time
round, a hint
at the melody
over skins and
tempered metal,
drums and cymbals,
cymbals and drums.

III.
He sings to
   the notes
he pulls
on the long, low,
thick strings: solo
on bass.

Improv

The tie guy in the subway station
shows us the way, which train,
says, "From Kansas? What do you do?"
and I say, "Professor. Poet," and he says,
"Tell me one," and I'm quiet, shy, but do,
recite "Bird's Horn," one of the only ones
I know by heart, smoothing the words
to him and the others in the subway car,
our hands clamped to the silver pole,
his head cocked my way, and he tells me
this is Parker's town, and I say,
"We claim him, too," bop genius
born in KCK, cut his teeth in KCMO,
his fast jazz sound
stretching to the coast
like a cigarette ghost,
like a long flat cirrus cloud,
like an unending river
coming from the mouth
of his golden golden saxophone.
Coltrane said he didn't hear
double-time till he heard Bird,
didn't know half
of the things you could do.

Neon Above All of the Clubs

This is Parker's town
   still, home of those
who can play
   fast fast
if they need to, bop,
   where fire
is respected, kept
   under ice
in whiskey
   and burns burns
above
   in neon tubes.

[that dance band]

That dance band,
   Slim Gaillard's, has
Parker on sax, though you
wouldn't know it, and is full
of absurd scat, including a bit
about how a motorcycle pops
   along. Is this what
people thought, lived
   through, this slough
of sound, like the scatted parts
   on *Inside Llewyn Davis*?
Something to eschew, if you
could, leave behind
that false shine, be a burnt
   or blackened penny,
never a new one. Leave those
   to the mint and those fat hands
outstretched at the printing
   and pressing machines.

"Poppity Pop" (Bulee "Slim" Gaillard)
LA, 29 Dec. 1945, BTJ40 / Bel-Tone 753

Bird at the Jelly Joint, Fall 1938
for Chuck Haddix

Only one photo
  of Bird
playing his horn
  in KC
is known, a shot
  taken by a student
for the U of KC yearbook
  at a casual gig, Bird
18, eyes closed
  reed at his teeth, lips
pensive. Behind him,
  the drummer's eyes
are also closed,
and he's playing
  with one hand,
the other stick
  in his mouth,
all out, no one
  from the local* here,
none to impress,
  so just play,
and so Jesse "Mad Drummer"
Price plays 111 choruses, an almost
  unending drum solo
over the novelty
  tune "Nagasaki," what
they want, what they
  dance to
this Café Society
of jitterbugs, out
after an afternoon
  nose to the black
board, chalk
  board, and dusty
musty books.

---

*local: musicians union, as in Local 34-627

Bird Watcher

Dean Benedetti, alto sax
   in a dance band,
went to gigs, recorded
only the solos, only
   Bird, live, in LA, like
a man in the woods
   with a mic
capturing birdsong.

It's said Benedetti
   quit sax,
sold drugs to keep
following, listening
hard for Bird.

Recording Bird from the Can

Benedetti arrives early
at the Dial date in Hollywood,
and the management says no mics,
   no cords, and so Benedetti
tacks an OUT OF ORDER sign
on one of the bathroom stalls,
   runs a discreet cord
to the front table spot
with a mic, and sits
   on the closed toilet seat,
machine cradled on his lap, headphones
   clamped to his ears.

Quote from Ross Russell: *Yardbird in Lotus Land*,
Chapter Two: Chez Billy Berg, published in *Le Jazz Hot*,
Jan. 1970, *Orkester Journalen*

at massey hall

more mosquito
  than bird
his solo
  on "all
the things
  you are"
on grafton
  plastic
saxophone

Bird's Table

Bird would sleep
   under the pool table
at Tootie's Mayfair
at 75/Wornall.
    When he
       went out, he
           went all out.

Bird at 100

It's the year Bird would have turned
   100, if he'd lived,
but he didn't. He lived
   fast, and didn't get the care
he needed, and used
   the needle and drank.
Bird said he'd give an "ulcer man . . .
   75 dollars to cool my ulcer,"
give a heart man 100 dollars to fix
   his heart, and none of it
worked, but he'd give
   "a little cat in a dark alley
five dollars for a bag of shit, (and)
   my ulcer's done, my heart trouble
(all) gone."

Quote from Chan Parker's *My Life in E-Flat*

[Sax Man]

When that
  sax man
leans back
  with his horn
he catches night
  by the neck
and willowy black mane,
  climbs,
climbs on.

At the Bar, Casey's

Jazz Drummer: You watch the news?

Bartender: I like to know what's going on in the world, and what's going on in my own country, which is really getting to be a drag, and Sue and I watch *Jeopardy* once in a while—and the Royals. This administration's getting me down, though. King Tang.

Lawyer: What'd I say after the elections? We'll be back. We're back! When you have time, will you send one of those fine young people up for two State Soups to go?

Jazz Drummer: I'm going out to see a play after. A friend wrote it. Wanna come?

Pianist: I hate to say it, but I don't see plays, unless I'm datin' an actor. But sure. Let's give it a whirl. Nudge me, if I drift off, though. Can you promise me that?

Open Mic with Music

That door hinge creak
a bass can make,
opens the door
for you.

[Older Drummer]

I had a stroke,
couldn't touch my nose,
had to work my way
back up
to single stroke rolls.

The Basie Way

There's this way
　of flattening out
the beat, while still
　swinging,
　　that Basie way,
DW taught us,
　how to chick
that hi-hat
　so that
it was like dancing—
　sidestep, sashay,
shuffle, a circle
　of shoes
on dance floor,
　and sand.

[how it ended]

That night, Cumulus kicked the tune
   a little too quickly, and we could barely
keep up, and I could hear everyone
   talking, every word, and had a hard time
entraining to the piano, and so unlike me
   I took a few pills, and my forehead burned,
and my sticks seemed to rumble
   over the drums and wash over
the cymbals without my brain
   saying anything, like I was dreaming
them into motion. I'd done this
   without pills forever when I was
better, when I was in shape, but I was
   way out of shape now, no longer gigging
for rent, but for fun, and I knew this could be
   a problem, and quit the pills, and quit
the gig, and let my drums sit silent
   Saturday nights, and took walks,
long walks at sunrise with my kid Sundays,
   pulled a red wagon behind me,
and not drums, and let the dust cover them up.

[Chops]

Once you've got
   chops, next
you need to learn
   to groove.

Tadd Dameron leaves a note
  by his photo:
"To Cliff—
    Don't B♭,
    Don't B#,
    Just B♮"

From a program for Festival International de Jazz, Salle Pleyel, Paris, 8 May-15 May, 1949

Growing Up

[swingset]

A swingset, its feet
trembling, and above and below
the chants and shrieks
of children.

Treasure

The toddler girl
  in her too-tall
stocking cap reaches
for something rustling
in the Walmart parking lot,
   pink paper and a flash
of silver. "Leave it,
  baby," says her mother.
"That's trash."

Walking Trail, Holiday Lights, Lenexa

When the little kid
   on the lit trail says,
     "Mommy, how do they
get all the lights
   up there?" Mom says,
"Squirrels. Lots and lots
   of trained squirrels."

23 Dec. 2018

When I Grow Up

Red says
   he wants to be
a metal bull rider
   or a preacher.
This is
   at church.
I say I'd like
   to make maps,
mark T's where
   I've been, maybe
walk like Jesus,
   sandals on sand.

Gifted

I didn't know
if I was slow or fast,
but they put me in that special class
with ham-handed Eddie
who used to try to beat me up
at black top's edge
each recess.

Donnie's always drumming
on his legs, on his chest,
always in trouble. Emily, too,
for dancing her feet
at her desk
to tunes no one hears.

Cosandra won't study
the class poems, says
none of them sound
like her.

Alex adds and subtracts, divides
for fun, but keeps forgetting
his worksheets, doesn't
turn them in.

Deandre's teacher
takes his open Pepsi
from his desk, tables it
by the board up front. So Deandre
takes her cup of tea and drinks.
Gets sent down the hall.

I hear teacher say,
"You're like a tribe
of wild horses, not completely out
of control, but always running,
running at full speed."

Pop Out King

When I kicked
　the red ball,
it'd always go
　up & up & up,
time enough
　for anyone
to get under it.
　I could round
third, & it'd still be
　up, & would get
caught, & I'd be out,
　almost home.

Fourth Grade

Rambler has Sally
  by the hands,
and he spins her in a circle
  above sandy blacktop,
and it looks
  like a game,
but is not, and he lets
  go, and Sally skids,
sand in her knees,
  and I go
and help her up,
  and she says,
Rambler and me,
  we were once
in love.

Dunked

Spindly held me
   shoulder blades tight
against his locker,
   while they dunked
Sam, head and hair
   in the gym toilet,
and in between dunks,
   I could hear
Sam's shouts, howls,
   and I kicked Spindly
in the nuts, and he dropped me,
but Sam was already out
and soaked and alone,
   and I put a hand
on his shoulder, helped
   him up.

About that time we left the locker room through a cloud

When Spindly held Sam up against the lockers, Spindly's fists at Sam's shoulders, pinning him, I thought of Spider-Man, how he would have cocked his legs and given Spindly a quick kick and sprung into the room, taken all of those pock-faced bullies out. Middle school was like that, bullies fighting their own faces—with razors and zit cream—then taking it all out on you, hoping to turn your face red, too. We learned to ball our fists when we heard our names. Don't wait. Don't get hit before you're ready to put at least one punch up, at least draw a purple bruise across a chin or chest, leave a mark before you go down. That way, you might not be the mark next time. That way, they know you have some scrap in you. We were all little. We were alone when gym was done, there in the locker room. The only time I saw coach stop a fight, all he did was turn all of the shower heads on. The room soon a cloud, and the little ones, we fled first from the plume, as if behind us there'd been fire or a bomb. We never looked back, not for fear we'd turn to salt, but because everyone knows you run better if you never ever turn.

[My pits itch]

My pits itch,
and I raise my arms to see
I've scratched until
there's a swarm of red spots
and scrapes. My father
also had this trouble,
worse, used only baby powder
under his arms, smelt
of gasoline and talcum
and the lawn, was never
mistaken for anything,
but a man.

Injured in Band

I used to knick my knuckles on the cymbal screws and drum hoop lugs, when I really played out in pep band, and I never had time to patch my hands, and so there'd be these little red dots on the white drum heads from when my hands went round the kit and from when I hauled into those cymbal rings, wobbling the golden dish like a bird wing flap-flapping. No one seemed to notice, until one night Cassandra helped me carry back my drums. We were halfway to the band room, when she licked her little finger and smeared one of those red dots.
    "That's blood, ain't it, Lip?" she said. "Your blood."
    "Sometimes I knick my knuckles," I said.
    "I guess sometimes you do." She leaned in a little closer, put a hand on my shoulder. "So, tell me, Lip. How's it hanging?" and I stammered, managed, "A little to the left." This always made her chuckle. She, along with the others, remembered how I'd racked myself striding diagonal across the football field in a new move, most of us wearing drum carriers struggling. In second hour Psych, I slid from my desk, said, "I need to see the nurse."

Guard

You could look out
  at the water
all day from the stand, think
anything, think nothing, watch
kids kick & swim & kiss,
& wonder: is this
all there is?

[handbill shot]

E was so little
when I ran
for School Board
with his small glasses
between our bodies
in our family shot.
I didn't win, but we kept
that picture. I cut it
from the handbills, sent it
to our friends.

Trampoline

Icy out. Lisa drives
Eliot downtown to bounce,
to fly above canvas and springs,
on the gym trampoline with kids
from his church. I keep
my phone on, close,
in case they
end up in the ditch.
I hate ice
and tires, driving
in this.

I remember how my niece said, "I didn't think he had it
in him," watching me float into the trees in her backyard
when I was 30, how she'd always seen me as too stiff to
rise above, to bend and kick my way into the clouds.

When our son grew old enough, we got one for our own
backyard, and my favorite part was lying on my back
on the tarp with my wife, clasping hands, looking up at
stars. We were not on the ground and not in the sky, but
resting above the bugs, above dirt, as if on a ship, sailing,
those points of light around the moon like guideposts
we once sailed to.

One year, the winds came, and that trampoline jumped
a chain-link fence and landed in someone else's
backyard. Our son grown, we left it where it landed.

Ready Player One

My son (15) has a little
   mustache, a wisp
of whiskers. He reaches up,
   adjusts his glasses, tells us
what he wants
   for Christmas: parts
to build his own
   new computer.
Through the door, through
   the wall, I can hear
his fingers tap through
   the keys, moving
a little man
   across the screen,
a little man who can
   fall and lift again, live
innumerable lives,
   unlike us
with only one, no
   restart, no "ready
player one."

[Inner Kid]

In my son's room, there are still dragons—in posters, made of clay and LEGOs. Although he's 15, a high school sophomore, there's still a bit of kid in him.

[our neighborhood]

No one in this neighborhood
 talks much; they just
bend to their flower beds
and push their mowers,
while the kids run
with the water guns.

[lugging]

And after I stop
　lugging drums, it gets
harder, my knees
　and arms, weak,
and the true test
　becomes carrying, not
playing across them.

Group Blast

Cool down, head
on the ground, and I look
up the blonde hardwood
floor to my wife at the front
and wonder: What
am I doing here? I can
never keep up.

My wife taught the class, Group Blast.

The Red Balloon
(Le ballon rouge, 1957)

At the end, the boy flies
tethered to a bundle of bright balloons
thick as grapes. They rise
over Belleville, the skin
of his red balloon ground-trampled, limp,
but the boy's spirit now
above the clouds.

Romance

Always Good

C.S. Lewis reminds us
   that some things
   are always good:
a waterfall, a rainbow,
two hands clasped.
   Take that away,
and you may never know
   that anything can be good.

Catherine & Hal

During the love scene
  in *Proof*, a guitar solo—

the party also
  going on
down below, the beer
bottles, mostly empty, held
  by the neck, brown
& green glass, like
the insulators
  used to hold
lightning, power lines
  high.

RE: The movie version of *Proof*, based on the Pulitzer Prize-Winning play by David Auburn

Rogue

Rogue's the one
  who can put you in a coma
    with a simple kiss, wants love, wears gloves.

And the Ring

Rebeck's got on
   a wide-brimmed hat
and new dress
   at the courthouse,
her hand in Bird's hand,
   though they don't yet
call him that, 15
   and she's marrying
a sax man, and Bird,
   he forgets the ring,
but his mother
   slips off hers,
lets them use that.

In the Pocket

Katie on bass, upright—
   tones so low
I have to stoop
to keep up
   on drums—

reminds me
   of that teen
jazz camp fantasy,
   being paired
with the only
rhythm girl
   so that keeping time's
like kissing, keeping
   time's like
holding hands—
   or more.

Hug

CJ & I play
Biz Markie, "Just
 a Friend" (1989), sit
on his front step, a pair
of orange muff
headphones between us, know
Anna Handle-Me will never
kiss me, touch me
except in
one goodbye
school's-over
hug.

Preacher Couple

We were both
  from West Texas,
cattle country, going
to college in liberal
Colorado. She lived
with vegetarians. Every once
in a while, we'd go
on a date, eat meat.

More Than Words

Kept on cassette
   in my white '67 Mustang fastback,
   Extreme's "More than Words,"
and I kept it on all
   June through August
when Summer dumped me, drove
   through those grey burb streets
slow with that song always on.

[say anything, or
  senior year break-up]

Back when I was in love,
I'd drive by Tamara's house,
just broken up, and stop at the curb
and wait just long enough
for a few breaths and a glimpse
of no one, then drive on, going nowhere.
I didn't raise a radio above my head,
boom our tune, and I only stopped
a couple of times and cried,
and I never ever saw her. No, that's
not quite right. I saw Tamara at my sister's
wedding, up on a mountain, a decade later.
And almost danced with her,
but didn't. I was married then,
and no longer dreamed
of high school, or long kisses
under Orion, just her hand
in my hand was all
I'd ever wanted, and a walk,
a long slow walk under the stars.

Sauce

Lisa's at the gym,
   and I'm cooking pasta.
I rub oregano between my fingers
like lathering soap, how
my ex-wife would
slow cook the sauce all day
with hand-ground spices, just
a taste, a touch, of that.

Lisa, my darling,
been writing poems
about our early love
in KC—here near our
"places," where we met and walked,
  hand in hand.

Plaza, Eastern Edge

Lisa lived here
   on this block, walked
the Nichols trail, past
   fountain and stoplight
and traffic always
   flowing, like breath,
like dark river water, and I grasped
her hand and took to the iced
sidewalk, took her
to look at books
   at Barnes and Noble, winters
when our love shined
like pressed pennies
the Feds make
   uptown, downtown,
wherever that is.

Happy Birthday

That afternoon, I wrote
a bday note, stuffed
a Hallmark card,
and signed my name, not
enough, so I wheeled
the Walmart aisles
for you, looking
for treasure under blue-
green fluorescent light, what,
what could you want?

Night Out, Away

My Dearest, I'm in a bar
  after a movie,
  drinking seltzer, thinking
of your hand in mine
at the Blue Room, a gin
and tonic in your hand,
at your lips, at my lips—
a flame   between us.

L on Piano

Those afternoons when Lisa
sits at the piano, even for 15 minutes,
remind me of why
I love her and are the best
ticking minutes of my life.
Even better, when
she sings, fingers
arpeggios across her guitar.
Music is what
some of us
were put here to do—
and if we're not flashy,
don't exhibit skin,
there's little place for us
except up in skyrises
or in aisle 2.

On Paper

Blue sky afternoon, and Lisa and I
catch a long table
by the window
in the coffee shop, and spread our dreams
across blonde tabletop,
song lyrics and poetic
sketches penned in blue
and green ink, and when
the songs come on
above, Muzak, we know
we have even bigger
dreams.

Sickness

[driving all night]

3 AM and I come off the highway
the loop, 635, and some guy
stops me on 16th Street, stands in traffic,
smacks his driver's license on my front window,
says, "It's me. It's really me,"
skinny, white, no shirt on, 20 or 30.
I drive on, slow, tell him no.

Andy's Blues

Russ says
　Sax Andy
stole from the store
and was fired, had a habit,
　　moved from music
store to music store
for years, then landed
　on the street in KC,
haven't heard from him.
"Sorry to hear it," I say;
"Sorry for the both of you."
Andy, he'd given me a CD,
　and I wanted
to pay him
　　or give it back.
No use
　　now.

How am I
any different? I take
pills the doctor orders,
and can't go long
　　without.

At the Short Stop Gas Station

Out goes the Which Wich,
and in comes the Dunkin' Donuts
from healthy veggies on bread
　to sugar—sprinkles
and glaze—and black coffee, pink
and orange sign, like neon
in the early morning,
like a lightning bug
butt, switching from on to off.

[corona—stage one]

so even our little town
goes mostly silent
at night, the only cars
parked at a diagonal
are outside mulready's pub,
people out for st. pat's day,
and I lug in my drums, play
like I've got a bodhran,
my brushes fluttering
over the drum
with the snares off,
and I try not to touch
anyone, but a fan or two
give us hugs, take hold
of a hand with that
double-fisted grasp.
I'm really not that famous,
just someone drunk
thinks they know me
and wants to touch.

[unintended birthday gift]

The neighbors have it,
   the pastor and his 6 kids,
held a bday party
   the night before
the lockdown started,
and now they've got it,
every single one.

[it's here]

Gray day, and the mourning dove
coos at noon. We watch
from the window, far from
the bug, though it's now in
our neighborhood, has kids
sick, and the old laid low.
If you listen closely early,
you can even hear the weeping.

[love in the time of coronavirus #1]

Lisa and I watch a bad movie, and after we hold hands, like two kids at the theater, like young lovers on her KC apartment couch. We don't know if the bug will pass over our house like a death angel, and so we remind ourselves it's just us here in this room this evening, our young son gaming in his own room, his fingers clicking over the keys, face bathed in blue computer light; no blood smeared over the doorway, it's just we three alone in this house, the wind outside like a monster, the streets all empty of cars.

[love in the time of the coronavirus #2]

A girl E liked
   asked him to prom,
and now, with the bug,
   prom is off, and there's
only so long E can stay home
   and game all day, before
he begins to notice
   everything he's
missing, everything
   he's lost.

[in our cave]

Do we grow more like
ourselves the longer
we stay inside, the longer
we wait, as if in a cave,
for this sickness to pass?

[the box]

I.
You can stop the TV,
get off your phone, and write.
It may hurt
to think, but you can.

II.
If you don't write
   or make songs
or paint, you have
   to go and live in some
other person's dream.

[how to work from home]

God, help me
   make it to
Noon, so I can sleep
   through my lunch hour,
while the others eat.

Sunday, 12 April 2020

I.
So quiet I can hear
   the clock tick.
Easter morning
  at home.

II.
No one goes
   to church
this Easter; stuck at home
because of the bug,
we watch the rain,
   the trees and grass
greening.

Cellphone, Palmed

We can watch
   nearly anything, hold
TV in our hands, look
   into that blue light
and see the past,
   the future, see anything,
but what rolls around us,
   like birdsong, like fire,
like star-shine, like that darkness
   that almost swallows the earth.

[how we use our space]

I.
I have a large yard,
   can go out
and walk across grass,
but do I?

II.
Feel the green
   beneath my feet. It's not
some sidewalk, some street.
It's not tallgrass, bluestem,
   but it's something.

[rumination]

Afternoons, I walk short circles
on our back patio. The neighbors
must think I've gone crazy, have lost it
to the bug, but I keep walking.
It will come to me
sometime. I know that it will.

[dying favor]

I ask you
   to take this cup
from me. I don't want
   to die alone
in a white room
   some Monday,
my lungs
   full, but
without
   a breath left.

[for George Floyd]

Tonight I watch George Floyd die, a cop atop
with a knee on Floyd's neck, Floyd's head
pressed into greying blacktop. Like with
an electrocution or lynching, we watch.
And do the white children point and call
and wonder at what's right? Just what
are we watching here? Is this how
America has always been
or is this how America finally dies?

[RE: the taunting of Nathan Phillips, Omaha Elder]

I've seen the video
  of those white boys
  in red hats
who surrounded the man
  with his drum
that smile they gave him—
  bully smile, smug, taunting
him to come to blows.
Teach me peace, Martin,
  teach me peace, Dr. King—
help me to stand
  with my brothers and sisters
  of color
when the red hats
  come, when
the red hats
  come to silence the drum.

Kobach on Parade

I was handing out maps at the Rotary table at Old Shawnee Days, the parade going by, and all of the sudden it gets deathly quiet, the kind of quiet when someone falls off a float or a horse goes down in the street, and we look, and Kobach's going by with his big gun mounted to a Jeep, and girls and boys are clinging to their mothers, grabbing hold of a leg or going under a skirt, and the Jeep wheels by like an anvil storm cloud, some wondering when the shooting will begin, the gubernatorial candidate waving, one hand on a machine gun, one hand in the air.

Kansas gubernatorial candidate and Secretary of State Kris Kobach rides in the Old Shawnee Days parade (3 June 2018) in a red, white, and blue painted Jeep with a nonfunctioning Browning M2 .50-caliber machine gun mounted on top.

Pitchforks

One: Those Democrats are gonna come with pitchforks.

Two: The only Democrats I've ever seen with pitchforks were composting.

Mom: When Jane Fonda came to Fort Hays State, the farmers did come into town with pitchforks. It was kind of a joke. She was touring the country and made a stop, a peace protest. And Dad was already in the Reserves and had to stave them off. And when we moved to KC, he had to guard the 18th Street Bridge, during the protests. In industrial arts, they were wanting to make knives and brass knuckles because of the race riots in the schools. It's a wonder why he didn't stay teaching, eh? The industrial arts trash cans were often on fire, and they were filled with wood and sawdust. Built a pretty good fire.

[hold on]

It's hard to say what
   will keep you going—
the stroke of fingers
   over keys or skin—
but whatever it is
   I ask you
to hold on.

Acknowlegdments

The author gratefully acknowledges Analog Submission Press for the first publication of the Charlie Parker "Bird" Poems in *Bird Book* (2020) as well as *Itty Bitty Writing Space* for the first publication of "Pitchforks" (2019) and *Poetrybay*'s publication of the pandemic poems "Sunday, 12 April 2020" and "[how we use our space]" (2020).

Thank you to the Emporia State University Provost's Office and Research and Grants Center, which helped support my research on the poems about Charlie "Bird" Parker found in this book.

Note

This symbol, seen on pages 40 and 96, is a coda symbol. In music, it signals the player to take a kind of special ending.

Current Influences

Musical:
Charles Mingus (*Ah Um*), Purna Loka Ensemble (*Metaraga*), Pat Metheny (*From This Place*), Bobby Watson, et al (*Bird at 100*), Bobby Watson (*Check Cashing Day*), Chick Corea (*Now He Sings, Now He Sobs*), Matthew Brewer (*Solo Conception*), Chris Hazelton's Boogaloo 7 (*Soul Jazz Fridays*), John Coltrane (*Both Directions at Once: The Lost Album*, *A Love Supreme*, and *Giant Steps*), Keith Jarrett Trio (*Standards Live*), Madeleine Peyroux (*Half the Perfect World*), Miles Davis (*Kind of Blue*), and Lisa Moritz (*Dream of Blue* and *Holding Time*), Jack DeJohnette, Rosanne Cash, Josh Ritter, Patty Griffin, Dollar Brand, Don Mumford, Gerald Dunn, Jackie Myers (*Clementine*), Brian Steever, Brandon Draper, Doug Auwarter, and Doug Talley.

Charlie "Bird" Parker: *The Complete Dean Benedetti Recordings of Charlie Parker*; *Charlie Parker: The Complete Savoy and Dial Studio Recordings, 1944-48*; *The Quintet: Jazz at Massey Hall*; and *The Essential Charlie Parker*.

Literary:
Tracy K. Smith (*Wade in the Water*), Stephen Karam (*The Humans*), Kevin Young (*Brown* and *Blue Laws*), Aimee Nezhukumatathil (*Oceanic*), Traci Brimhall (*Rookery*), Tasha Haas (*Certain Dawn, Inevitable Dawn* and *The Garden of Earthly Delights*), Chuck Haddix (*Bird: The Life and Music of Charlie Parker*), Ben Lerner (*The Topeka School*), Dale Carnegie (*How to Win Friends and Influence People*), Napoleon Hill (*How to Think and Grow Rich*), Ta-Nehisi Coates (*Black Panther*), *The Amazing Spider-Man* (Vol. 1, #302, July 1988), Stanley Crouch (*Kansas City Lightning: The Rise and Times of Charlie Parker*), Walt Whitman (*Leaves of Grass*), *The Portable Beat Reader* (ed. Ann Charters), Jack Kerouac (*The Subterraneans*), The Pocket Meiser Eckhart, Sarah Ruhl

(*The Oldest Boy*), Rhonda Byrne (*The Secret*), Kay Ryan (*The Niagara River*), Cornel West (*Democracy Matters*), Susan Hill (*The Woman in Black*), Reisner (*Bird: The Legend of Charlie Parker*), Tim Wise (*White Like Me...*), Jonathan Holden (*Knowing*), Terence Rattigan (*Flare Path* and *The Deep Blue Sea*), Albert Camus (*The Plague*), Tyehimba Jess (*Olio*).

Film & TV:
Born to Be Blue, Chasing Trane, Miles Davis: Birth of the Cool, Miles Ahead, Da 5 Bloods, and *The Big Bang Theory* (the final season).

Words of Thanks

Thanks to Linzi Garcia for all of her help curating this manuscript. Thank you to Tracy Million Simmons for believing in this project and publishing this book. Thank you for Lisa Moritz, love of my life. Thanks to Eliot Rabas, a fine and upstanding young citizen. Thanks to my parents, Gary and Joyce Rabas, for helping raise me right. Thanks to the following for writing glowing and illuminating blurbs for this book: Michael D. Graves, Silvia Kofler, Ronda Miller, Tyler Sheldon, and Sir Michael Miller. Thank you to a few special folks, including Steve Catt, Mel Storm, Amy Sage Webb Baza, Ray Lauber, Jacob Brittain, and Richard Warner. Thank you to my many friends and fans, far and wide. And thanks to you for picking up this book.

Past Poet Laureate of Kansas (2017-2019) Kevin Rabas teaches at Emporia State University, where he leads the poetry and playwriting tracks and chairs the Department of English, Modern Languages, and Journalism. He has fourteen other books, including *Lisa's Flying Electric Piano*, a Kansas Notable Book and Nelson Poetry Book Award winner. He is the recipient of the Emporia State President's and Liberal Arts & Sciences Awards for Research and Creativity, and he is the winner of the Langston Hughes Award for Poetry. His plays have been performed across Kansas and on both coasts.

If you enjoyed what you read, please consider contacting the author.

Kevin Rabas
PO Box 274
Emporia, KS 66801

kevinrabas1@gmail.com
kevinrabas.com

Meadowlark Press
— since 2014 —

meadowlark-books.com

www.ingramcontent.com/pod-product-compliance
Lightning Source LLC
Chambersburg PA
CBHW072202100526
44589CB00015B/2336